THERE MUST BE MORE

DENNIS GOLDSWORTHY-DAVIS

Published by Open Wells Ministries

15315 Capital Port, San Antonio, Texas 78249

ISBN: 978-1-7355716-6-9

DEDICATION

I dedicate this book to those who have gone on before me that changed my life and prospective. My Pastor Bennie Finch, who drove me to chase God, Bob Main who carried such an anointing and so many others. I also dedicate this book to those who will not sit complacent in their walk with God. Go for it my friends! You won't be disappointed.

Contents

OTHER BOOKS BY

DENNIS PAUL GOLDSWORTHY-DAVIS

Available on Amazon.com

Grace Looks Good on You

Touching the God of Jacob

Standing in the Perfect Storm

Gaining the Commanded Blessings

Unlimited Anointing: Secrets to Operating in the Fullness of God's Power

Walking in the Prophetic

Grabbing the Heel of Destiny

Don't Take the Bait

FOREWORD

BY ROBERT HENDERSON

I remember my pastor, telling me the story concerning how he was baptized in the Holy Spirit. He was a Baptist pastor for at least two decades. He had however gotten very dissatisfied with his spiritual walk and life in God and ministry. He had actually said to the Lord, "If this is all there is, then I can't do it anymore." He wasn't speaking of his relationship with the Lord, but what he was experiencing in ministry. He had just hit the bottom and simply was at the point of burn out and emptiness. At this place, a man walked up to him in a garage where he was having his car repaired. He began to witness to my pastor about the person and power of the Holy Spirit. My pastor said that at this point, he thought the man was crazy. However, within a few days, he was looking for him. He did find him and ended up receiving the baptism of the Holy Spirit through the ministry of a Spirit-filled couple in the city where they lived. Everything changed because of this experience. He actually got kicked out of the Baptist church he had started. He went on though, to a fruitful ministry and discipleship of other ministers. This all happened because he became hungry for more. When we make the statement, "There must be more", we are declaring a hunger for God. We are not accusing God of lack or insufficiency. We are actually reaching and desiring something that only He can provide. Sometimes God will allow us to come to the end of ourselves, so He can fill us with Himself. This is what Deuteronomy 8:3 tells us that God purposely allowed the children of Israel to hunger, so that He could then fill them.

So, He humbled you, allowed you to hunger, and fed you with manna which you did not know nor did your fathers know, that He might make you know that man shall not live by bread alone; but man lives by every word that proceeds from the mouth of the Lord. Before the Lord gave them what they did not know, He allowed them to become hungry. This is almost always the case. The Lord will create a hunger in us that we have never known. This is so that He might fill us with that which we also have never known. In fact, this verse says that what God fed them with, even the previous generation had not known. I believe we are living in a day, when God is unlocking that which has been reserved for this day. There is that which God has kept back for this time of history. It will be those who are looking for it, that will become the porthole that God pours it through. The result will be a manifestation of glory that is for this day. We will find a resounding "Yes there is" to the statement of "There must be more!"

Robert Henderson
Best-Selling Author of "The Court of Heaven" series

EVER INCREASING ANOINTING

A few years back I wrote a book when the Lord spoke to me to teach people on the Anointing's of God. Its purpose was to cause us to look at the spectrum of anointing and its great realm that we could all touch and walk into. I never for a moment thought that it would open the door for the Lord to start showing me more in this realm than I had first discovered or even imagined. I was quite amazed when He talked to me again saying that we all needed to see that anointing can be increased and increased. You will see once we look more into it that we can either be touched by the anointing in a light measure or can walk in it to a place of overflow like Peter did in Acts 5.

<u>GOD IS NO RESPECTER OF PERSONS</u>

It is so easy to fall into the trap that multitudes have done through the ages. That God's promises and provisions are for the few rather than all His sons and daughters. Yes, I know that we all would nod our heads to the truths but don't know how affected by culture and sometimes Christian TV we are. Some of us grew up in cultures where there was 'them' and 'us'. But who are "they"? To so many "they" are the aristocracy while to others the ultra rich. It's what we perceive to be the superheroes of the faith like the early church, Paul, and certain characters of history whose names are bounded about by many church members. Perhaps it's even the professional clergy and fivefold ministry according to Ephesians 4. No, my friends! As you soon will discover in this book, the anointing in all its fullness is for all!

THE SPIRIT OF CHRIST

We are told in Romans 8:9, that without the Spirit of Christ, we don't belong to Him. Notice it says the Spirit of Christ, not just the Spirit of Jesus. The Spirit of the anointed one! Several verses later in Romans 8:11, we are told, "if the Spirit of him who raised Jesus from the dead." The same Spirit meaning the same anointing given to all that believe in and receive Him! The same, not different, not lesser or watered down. No, the same! The same power, the same potential and the same fullness that inhabited Christ is now given to us. Once we see the potential and all that it means for us, all things are possible!

A REVELATION IS NEEDED

Paul tells the Ephesians of his continued prayer for revelation for them (Eph. 1:17-19 ESV). In other words, he had seen it and walked it, but now was praying that they could too. We need to catch parts of verses 18 and 19 that state, "having the eyes of your heart enlightened ... is the immeasurable greatness of his power toward us who believe." It will make a difference to the reading of this book and honestly, to the results as well.

The next verse tells us that it is the power that was exercised when he raised Christ from the dead (see Eph. 1:20). This is the power available towards us and for us. Although, without seeing it we will never desire it, expect it, or try to walk into it! The purpose of this book is to help enlighten what is available. Better yet, it is to stir our hearts to want to run toward it with a desire to gain it for ourselves.

CHAPTER 1

THERE HAS TO BE MORE

THE ANOINTING MAKES A DIFFERENCE

Ever since I was born again in a British Pentecostal church in January of 1973, I have been fascinated by the anointing! The fascination actually started when the Lord, who called me to preach very soon after I was saved, suddenly anointed me to do so. I had tried to preach for the first time, clearly without the anointing. He suddenly anointed me in a moment, and I ministered the same message a second time within about 24 hours, but oh the difference. The anointing makes all the difference! It enables us to do what we cannot do without it. You have only to read of the results of the day of Pentecost in Acts Chapter 2 to see this same experience when the 120 were filled and anointed by the Holy Spirit. The anointing makes the difference!

INCREASED MEASURES

As I continued in my quest to know the anointing, I realized that God is a God of measures. You find this recorded in Ephesians 3:19 when speaking of the love of God. It changes the measure in which you are filled with God. Once again, in Ephesians 4:13 it speaks of gaining the whole measure of the fullness of God. This means there are measures that we can reach and walk in with the intention of walking in the fullness of God. Paul said he reached this goal in Romans 15:29. "I know that when I come to you, I will come in the full measure of the blessing of Christ." Whoa! The full measure? Yes, he reached it and so can we as God is no respecter of persons! Truthfully, if we are to grow up into Christ according to Ephesians 4:15, then we are to grow into all that He was and is. He was given the Spirit without measure (John 3:34 ESV), which means without limits. He received the fullness of the measure of anointing! So, if we are to be "conformed to the image of his son" as Romans 8:29 says, then the intention of the Lord is to bring us to the *full measure* just as he did with Paul!

If you have ever read Ezekiel 47 and the description of the river of God, it is so clear that it increases in measure. First it is ankle deep, then knee deep and waist deep and then the waters flow beyond ability to stand in and yet the prophet was in the middle of it. The ever increasing flow of the depth of the anointing is available to all who desire to be led further up this river just like the prophet (Ezekiel 47:1-12).

MAKING IT OURS

The intention in every chapter of this book is to stir our desires and lead us to a deeper and richer anointing. Always remember, "he who began a good work in you will carry it on to completion until the day of Christ

Jesus," (Philippians 1:6). He wants us to walk in the fullness of Christ! In fact, the full quote of Romans 8:29 has verse 28 added. "All things God works for the good of those who love him, who have been called according to his purpose." What purpose? Now add in verse 29 which states that this purpose is for us to be "conformed to the image of his son." The word image used there in the original language is that of being in like manner and expression. Yes, it is God's intention and His predetermined purpose. It is His declared purpose, but we also must become involved and must make it ours! We must seek it and chase it and follow it. Ever increasing anointing! It is our portion and our calling and God's manifest purpose for us.

STIRRED BY DESIRE

That beautiful song that comes from Psalm 42:1 springs to mind. "As the deer pants after the water brooks." The desire for all that God has for us must become such a longing that it will drive us into action. The action that will stop at nothing to be fulfilled and until we become fully filled.

THERE HAS TO BE MORE FOR ME

Have you ever made this cry, "There has got to be more!" Oh yes you have and so have I, but this book is here to show you there is more and it is on offer! But our cry has got to change to, "I want more, and I am going to have more because that is my inheritance too."

CHAPTER 2

THE ANOINTING DEPICTED

STAGES OF THE RIVER

What a beautiful picture of the anointing that is seen in Ezekiel 47. It shows the river of God from its commencement through to its fullness. From verse 2 through 6, Ezekiel was led up the river until it reached its height and full flow. It shows us clearly that the river increases as it goes and also that the purpose of God is to take us to fullness. Hence, being led up the river.

The different stages of the river, which have been explained by so many great preachers, show the deeper the depth, the greater the influence. Let's look at the different realms:

A.) Ankle deep - Ezekiel 47:3

Clearly the river is deep enough to walk in, wade in and splash in, but not really deep enough for fish or fishing. This is when the river has affected our walk, which is essential, but is not deep enough to do much more. So many like this place in the river. A place of feeling, enjoyment and thrill, but the fruit is further up the river. So, let's name ankle deep as the place of the thrill of the river!

B.) <u>Knee deep</u> – Ezekiel 47:4

This is when the river affects our intimate life. The river's current is now stronger and deeper. Not quite the place to frolic but affecting our affections, prayer life and worship. Beginning to change our whole lifestyle to that of a heart towards holiness and piety. Again, many stay here because they love the place of intimacy and closeness, yet there is more, as we see in the same verse.

C) <u>Waist deep</u> - Ezekiel 47:4

Waist deep is a beautiful place because it is where the river affects the inner man. It's a place where the river begins to flow out of us, as Jesus promised (John 7:37-38). A place of knowing the flow of the Spirit and anointing. Beginning to touch and minister to others and for many this is a purpose fulfilled place. What more can we need than this? Surely we are ministering now as Jesus did, but God wants us in a higher measure than even this, so the prophet is lead further. Now let's name the waist deep stage as the place of ministry in the river.

D) <u>Waters to swim in</u> - Ezekiel 47:5

Wow, what place is this? A place too deep to be in control. A place where the river is in control, and we cannot even stand up. Indeed, a place where the river is the overwhelming flow and runs the direction of our lives and ministries. It's here in verse 6 that the prophet is asked, "do you see this?" A place where the waters touch your sight, and you see as God wants you to see and touch the whole of your body and being. In verse 7 he suddenly sees the trees alongside the river. The prophetic from heaven opens and he sees what the river does in its fullness.

THE RIVER MEASURED

As we read this portion of scripture, we are told that the man who leads him measures the river out, then leads him deeper and further in this river. That is the Lord's intention. To take us from measure to measure, from fullness to greater fullness and from glory to glory. There is more in the river if we let ourselves be led further and further into its fullness. Jesus said to the original disciples in Matthew 4:19 (KJV), "Follow me, and I will make you fishers of men." The key is to follow where we are led, and we will reach our preordained potential. There is a danger we all face the moment we touch and are touched by the river. We feel this can suffice rather than the fulfillment of being fully immersed in this river of God.

CHAPTER 3

WHY NOT ALL AT ONCE

Why don't we receive all the fullness of God at once?
Why are there stages?

CHILD TO ADULT

Paul gives us a clear depiction of growth in God in
Galatians 4:1-2. "What I am saying is that as long as
heir is underage, he is no different to a slave, although
he owns the whole estate. The heir is subject to
guardians and trustees until the time set by his father."

What a tremendous depiction of growth. You own it all
but are not ready for it all! Just like with children, as
they grow, they can be entrusted with more. We grow
from spiritual babes to adults. 1 John 2:12-14 clearly
depicts this. We read of:

- Children
- Young men
- Fathers

A young man can be given far more responsibility than
a child can. But a father? Now that is a person that is
mature enough to handle it all.

MATURITY IS TRUSTED

James 1:4 says, "Let perseverance finish its work so that you may be mature and complete, not lacking anything." Clearly maturity in God can be trusted with anything and is trusted with everything. As God by his Spirit matures us, then He is able to entrust us. To be mature enough to handle the dynamite of the anointing, to know how to minister it and not become proud or arrogant because they are so filled. The context is quite amazing because it says maturity comes with perseverance. The walk has been proven and the race has been run and now a place of trust has been reached!

FAITHFUL IN A LITTLE

Jesus, when giving the parable of the talents, shows us that everything is about faithfulness. "Well done, good and faithful servant! You have been faithful with a few things; I will put you in charge of many things." (Matthew 25:23)

In Matthew 25:30, we are clearly shown that we are tested by being given portions from God. How we respond to these tests enables Him to entrust us with more. A little anointing, a specific charge or a gift to operate in will open the door for more, or sadly less, as the parable teaches us. We need to understand the ways of God. How can I walk in fullness if I won't even be faithful with less?

PROMOTED BEYOND CAPABILITY

Have you ever heard the statement, "We are promoted to our level of capability?" What this means is that even in the world's system they will try to get you to your highest place of competence, but beyond that you might dismally fail! We are not of the world, but the Lord will also never take us beyond our ability to fulfill. The difference being that He will work on us and in us until we become able to reach greater potential and carry greater depth. A great scripture on this is found in Ps 66:10-12. We will be:

- Refined as silver.
- Squeezed in on every side.
- Men riding over our heads.
- Tested by fire and water.
- But then, ENLARGEMENT!

It seems clear that when refined and tested we become able to carry, do and flow much more!!.

CHAPTER 4

BEING LED STEP BY STEP

Here is good news for the hungry! Ezekiel was led step by step into the depths of God. In fact, Romans 8:14 (KJV) speaks of this saying, "For as many as are led by the Spirit of God, they are the sons of God." It is the ministry of the Holy Spirit to lead us into the fullness of our inheritance according to the verses surrounding Romans 8:14. In verse 17 it speaks clearly of the fact that we are heirs of and co-heirs with Jesus. It means the Lord wants to lead us into full measure. The measure of Jesus Himself! That's what co-heirs means; to inherit equal to.

THE NEED TO FOLLOW

We need to know that leading requires following. Jesus Himself told the disciples to, "Follow me, and..." (See Matt 4:19). The "and" is what follows the following. If we will respond to the leading and working of the Spirit, He will fulfill his purpose. We are told clearly in Galatians 5:25 that it is our job to, "keep in step with the Spirit." He will lead us to fullness, but we must follow. There is a famous statement made about a certain famous soccer manager that says, "He knows how to park the bus." What on earth does that mean? It means to shut it all down and lock the team in defense with no more forward motion. Sadly, I think many

Christians have parked the bus due to wanting a life of ease or wanting to go no further than they have to, thus never fulfilling their God given purpose. The Lord once told me that even in our home congregation there were those who had said, "This far and no further!" How sad it was for me as a leader to hear that, but can you imagine heaven's sadness when people have decided what milestone they will stop at?

DRAW ME AND....

The Song of Solomon has a wonderful verse in chapter 1:4. "Draw me after you; let us run." It seems, from this great verse, that in order to follow there is the need of desire! I believe the Spirit of God will woo, draw and stir us continually. After all, He is called to lead us to be fulfillments of Romans 8:29 that says we are, "predestined to be conformed to the image of his Son!" Let's be real though, *I will run after you* is a whole lot of desire. It's like the desire mentioned in Psalms 42:1(KJV) that says, "As the hart panteth after the water brooks." So hungry and so thirsty that it causes far more action than the normal. It's that action and thirst that cause David to have such an anointing and revelation. It's that same action that made Paul press in after God in Phil 3:12. Actually, the word used there in the Greek is like that of hounding and hunting until the desire be fulfilled.

USING MEN TO AWAKEN US

The New Testament adds several great thoughts of how the Lord gets us to the desired place. Galatians 4 speaks of setting us under guardians and trustees until we can fully inherit. This really means God uses spiritual fathering to lead us to all He wants. He wants you to follow those who ran before! In Ephesians 4:1-16 He uses the ascension gift ministries to also equip us to such a place. God will lead you to fathers and God will lead you to be under an ascension gift ministry that will connect with other ministries to bring you to fullness! (You just gotta read that passage). If your leaders aren't taking you to fullness, ask the leader of the church to place you where they will!

FAST TRACK

So, my friends, let's cry out in desire and never miss a step which the Lord has for us. When I travel abroad, I often get given the fast track to go through the airport system. Let's cry out for our fast track! "Draw me! We will run after you!" (Songs 1:4 AMP)

CHAPTER 5

ANOINTED IN STAGES

DAVID AND ELISHA - GREAT EXAMPLES

Have you ever read the life of David or the mantling of Elisha? It will become apparent very quickly that they were anointed in stages. Elisha was touched by the mantle in one encounter found in 1 Kings 19:19. Then in another encounter in 2 Kings 2, he was able to fully possess the same mantle. The journey of it is in the whole chapter. David was actually anointed three different times. The original anointing was when Samuel anointed him unto kingship in 1 Samuel 16:13 and then again in 2 Samuel 2 where he was anointed by Judah to be their king. Finally, Israel anointed him to be king. Watch the progression:

- Anointed to be King.
- Anointed as King of one tribe.
- Anointed to be King of a whole nation.

It happens in three separate stages.

ANOINTED AND THEN ANOINTED

How many times do we read of Peter being anointed in the book of Acts? There is the famous outpouring of Acts 2, which is so foundational to the birth of the church and to the truth of the baptism of the Spirit. We cannot fail to see the importance of Acts 4:31, where the anointing went just from them being filled into a room shaking experience. Acts 2 is about being individually filled but Acts 4 takes us to another level. You will also read of another anointing in between these in Acts 4:8. Finally, if you read Acts 5 this anointing is no longer contained within the body and Peter's shadow starts to heal (see Acts 5:15-16). What a realm of the anointing!

EVER INCREASING ANOINTING

Yes, *ever increasing anointing*, in the early church, and *ever increasing anointing in the Old Testament.* But look at who God anoints! He chooses a farmer, a shepherd and then a fisherman! They are just ordinary people, but people that the Lord knew would use their anointing on behalf of God for others!

STRENGTH TO STRENGTH

We must never settle for anything less than fullness! We should look for the staging points of God as we follow his step-by-step journey into this fullness. Psalms 84, which is one of my favorite psalms, in verse 7 speaks of us going from strength to strength. This means from staging post to staging post, encounter to encounter and experience to experience! This means fresh touches, visions and ownership and the list could go on and on. In Psalms 84:5, this promise belongs to a group of people that look to the Lord for their strength. It tells us that He sets the journey in their hearts to those who do such a thing. In fact, one version says, "'Who set their hearts on pilgrimage!" What a wording! The journey is on and the destination is set! For such a people, no valley and no tears will hinder this process.

Psalms 84:5-7 says, "Blessed are those whose strength is in you, whose hearts are set on pilgrimage. As they pass through the Valley of Baka, they make it a place of springs; the autumn rains also cover it with pools. They go from strength to strength, til each appears before God in Zion." What a journey He has placed in our hearts if we love the glory, the power and the anointing of God!

CHAPTER 6

WHAT KIND OF BAPTISM OF THE SPIRIT

SPRINKLED OR FILLED

I remember such a significant revelation concerning the infilling of the Spirit known as the Baptism of the Spirit. Just after I was truly born again, my pastor had said to me that I needed to be baptized. My answer was, 'No! I was baptized as a child in the church of Ireland! ' I will never forget his answer. "That wasn't baptism, that was a sprinkling!" The difference between a touch and immersion. This is the same when it comes to the baptism of the Spirit; how great was your baptism? Was it fully immersed, partially immersed or just touched? The actual word used for baptism is a Greek word Baptizō, which actually means to be overwhelmed or to make whelmed which is fully wet. Depending on the depth of baptism is how fully wet you are. Many speak in tongues and feel that they have the full package. Surely the full package is much more in the realm of overwhelming, where you are hidden in that which overwhelms you? Like in Ezekiel 47:6 where the river is too deep to be in control, but the river is in control.

CONSTANT INFILLING

Now let's look at another rendering of this Greek word. Thayer's Greek lexicon shares the statement, "to dip repeatedly." This is not a solo event but a repeated one, as the early church proves where the Holy Spirit filled them repeatedly. You see this referenced in Acts 2:4 and then again in Acts 4:8. There's also an incredible encounter in Acts 4:31 which was so powerful that the room shook. It says in verse 33 that, "Great grace was upon them all," (KJV). This last one caused Peter's shadow in Acts 5:15 to heal people without being touched. He had touched people in Acts 3 but now his shadow? Rooms shaking? *A greater depth indeed!*

DIFFERING MEASURES

Paul, as mentioned in the introduction, clearly knew differing measures. To say that he would come in the full measure meant that he had experienced those measures, or he would not have referenced it at all. He, like Peter, knew the ongoing and ever growing depth of the Spirit of God within his walk. It stirs me writing it as my spirit reaches out for more and yet more!

GROWING IN OUR MEASURES

Why not all at once? That's a fair question and worth a chapter in this book. Simply, we need to grow into our measures as we grow in Christ. This is spoken of so well in Ephesians 3:16-20. The greater the grasping of Christ, the greater measure we can walk in.

The father wants us to have all as it is our inheritance as seen in Romans 8:17. In Acts 2:33 Jesus released his fullness and the Holy Spirit sought to reveal and move us in to the fullness of it. Galatians 4:5 speaks of His wrestling with us for such things.

Don't be satisfied with a sprinkling or just one immersion, but rather let us be baptized again and again such as the early church was. If Paul and Peter can have it and people in history can have it, so can we. We have got to have it and must have it! No selling ourselves short!

CHAPTER 7

FILLED WITH ALL THE FULLNESS

Where did you get that statement from? Well, it's a statement that comes from a scripture in Ephesians 3:19. The whole context is quite amazing. "For this reason, I kneel before the Father, from whom the whole family in heaven and on earth derives its name. I pray that out of his glorious grace he may strengthen you with power through his Spirit in his inner being, so that Christ may dwell in your hearts through faith. And I pray that you, being rooted and established in love, may have power, together with all saints, to grasp how wide and long and deep is the love of Christ, and to know this love that surpasses knowledge- that you may be filled to the measure of all the fullness of God." Ephesians 3:14-19 NIV 1984 version.

So in Verse 16, we are told that we are strengthened by the Spirit in the inner being in order that:

1. Christ may dwell in our hearts by faith.
2. We might be rooted and grounded in love (Not just any love but that Agape love which is sacrificial and a manifestation of the love of Christ).
3. We may be able to seize with all the saints its fullness.
4. We might know intimately this love (Love that is experienced, not just a head knowledge).

5. The result being we are able to experience the fullness of God.

FAST TRACK TO FULLNESS

Honestly? Once again, a fast track to His fullness. Why? Because when we experience and grasp the love of Christ in its fullness, we can be trusted with the same fullness that Jesus Himself had. Our motive and heart is to minister the same way that the Lord did and does. This makes us want to ask the Holy Spirit for His strength and ministry in us completely. Strengthen me Lord so that! Reveal the fullness of the love of Christ, so that!

INCLUDES US ALL

We have to take a second look at verse 18 where it says, "With all the saints." This is not just for the one or two, but this is for all saints to experience and grasp. The result being that all saints can be filled to his fullness. This is not exclusive to the few and it is not exclusive to ascension gift ministries. No! This is an all saint's promise.

TAKING HOLD OF

Now let's look closer at the Greek word used to hold. It is the word Katalambanō, which means to take hold of, to seize and possess. Quite simply, the Holy Spirit will reveal it by revelation, but we must become spiritually aggressive in grabbing and not letting go until we own and possess what is revealed and offered.

APPREHEND ALL THAT IS OFFERED

Quite honestly, this scripture seems quite shocking. Think about it! The intention of God is that all saints can know and experience the fullness of God's love and can then be filled with His fullness. The question is, will all saints apprehend such a thing? Historically, the answer is no they won't, but that doesn't stop you and me. Once we know about a truth, then we must make it our aim or goal to possess such a truth until it becomes ours. Through the years we can see saints that did apprehend it. Their names are common to us, such as Smith Wigglesworth and Kathryn Kuhlman. If we check their histories out, they are just like us. They are quite normal and had their own issues that they walked, but they did what was offered and reached in to touch a love that led to the fullness of the life of God. Again, historical records show the results of such lifestyles, but to once again remind us that this is an all saints' promise. If they can do it, then I can do it and so can you. The promise belongs to all of us, but the response and prayer is ours. They are just historical markers to push us further in our journey to fullness.

CHAPTER 8

THAT I MIGHT GAIN CHRIST

Now here is a statement worth following! This is Paul in his pursuit for more of what he has begun to experience in God. In fact, in Philippians 3:7-8 he states, "But whatever were gains to me I now consider loss for the sake of Christ. What is more, I consider everything a loss because of the surpassing worth of knowing Christ Jesus my Lord, for whose sake I have lost all things. I consider them garbage, that I may gain Christ."

TO GAIN IS TO WIN

To gain is to win and to own as one's own! Paul's desire was to fully gain the anointed one. The journey here reminds us of Elisha who was touched by the mantle and wouldn't stop until he gained it for himself. So Paul, touched by the Lord, says everything else is as nothing or no value. I must have it all! I must own as my own! To gain has desire and grasping and receiving within it. It reminds us of an athlete desiring to win the crown as in the Olympics. In his writing Paul speaks of this in 1 Corinthians 9:24-27. Let me paraphrase this passage. I don't run aimlessly or fight like one punching into the air, on the contrary, I am after the prize, I am running to win! This is the attitude of a gainer. He sees what is possible and reaches to grab it, whatever the cost is.

THE KINGDOM OF HEAVEN SUFFERS VIOLENCE

Once again this brings us to Jesus 'great statement when speaking of the Kingdom of Heaven. In Matthew 11:12 (ESV) it says, "From the days of John the Baptist until now the kingdom of heaven has suffered violence, and the violent take it by force." Wow, what an awesome analogy of a gainer!

• John the Baptist declares what is coming.

• Men hear the sound of this voice.

• They run to its sound.

• They grab and grasp what is on offer until they possess it.

Indeed, this is an analogy of a gainer. However, when you hear it or see it you become stirred. Something within you goes after it until you gain it and own it. This is far from the picture of Christians that so many preach of, which is the passive believer who is moved by nothing. Rather it's a believer stirred into action and desiring to gain all that has been offered! In this case it's the fullness of Christ and the fullness of the anointed one. Gosh, even writing this my passions and affections are stirred!

THE SOUL FOLLOWING HARD AFTER GOD

You see this again and again in the Psalms. I thirst and I long, therefore ... (Psalms 63:1-8). Verse 8 actually speaks of David sharing that his soul followed hard after God, like that of a hunter pursuing its game until it gains its pursuit (KJV). To gain is active and aggressive in its quest! A gainer will not be denied, indeed like a hunter or like an athlete desiring his crown.

TO RECEIVE IS TO GAIN

In fact, the basic Greek word used for the word receive in the New Testament has this same thought within. It is the Greek word, 'Lambano,' which in interpretation means to see that which is offered and to reach out to take it and *gain it.* Christ, in his fullness, is on offer. Our stance, like David and others, is to want to gain like Elisha who reached down and picked up the mantle of Elijah in 2 Kings 2:12. It's one thing to see a truth or a promise but another to reach out to gain it. Oh, God of Elisha and David and of the early church, don't let me go until I gain that which is mine!

CHAPTER 9

DESIRE DRIVES US

When I was a young man, I fell for this girl who lived on the other side of our city. In fact, I think it was nearly 5 miles away. I had no car and not too much money, (there were no cell phones or FaceTime then) so to get to see her I had to either walk or run from where I lived. She came out of her house about 8:00 AM to walk to work. So, in order to be there I had to set out really early and run down the hill that we lived on, through the valley and back up on the other side, all by 8:00 AM. Wow, are you nuts? No, desire drove me! Later, after I got saved and my car broke down, I did the same to get to the early morning prayer at 6:00 AM. It was about 4 miles. What?! Now we know you are nuts. NO! Desire drove me! When there is desire and passion, all things are possible, and nothing is too much. Desire will drive us to the next level. In fact, God uses desire to move us. Listen to the words of David in Psalm 63:1, "earnestly I seek you; I thirst for you, my whole body longs for you." He was clearly driven by the desire within his heart.

PAUL'S INSATIABLE THIRST

It is this desire that Paul speaks of in Philippians 3. This chapter is filled with desire, particularly verses 7-14. Paul speaks of his first encounter with knowing Christ. In verse 8 he tells us that everything was dung compared to that, but it stirred within him a desire for more, which is clearly shown throughout the ensuing verses. It is quite compelling and stirring to say the least. Phil 3:12 is imperative to our gaining more in God! Let me quote again this key verse of Paul's insatiable desire. "Not that I have already obtained all this, or have already arrived at my goal, but I press on to take hold of that for which Christ Jesus took hold of me." Then in verse 14 such a key statement is made. "I press on toward the goal to win the prize for which God has called me heavenward in Christ Jesus." Paul is arguably the most anointed man in the New Testament and maybe of all that have come after him and he tells us what caused him to get there. Desire my friends, desire! Stirred up and possessed by desire and following his desire until he gained it all.

STIRRED BY THE SPIRIT OF DESIRE

The Holy Spirit will stir desire in us. A desire that cannot be satisfied with staying where we are. Clearly, I think that Galatians 4:5 speaks of this. Its translation means that the Spirit stirs and groans to fulfill our destiny that He has started to work in us. We must be careful that we don't quench such a desire but, rather like Paul and David, won't stop until we gain all that God has intended to give us. Proverbs 13:12 makes such a statement. "A longing fulfilled is a tree of life." That is a Holy Spirit wow. It clearly means to awaken in us that longing or desire. It makes us touch nothing less than the tree of life itself!

38

WHEN WE LOSE OUR DESIRE

We are clearly warned in Ecclesiastes 12:5 that there can be a time when desire is no longer stirred. Obviously in the context it means when men are about to go to their eternal home. Yet the truth of this statement is that when we are no longer stirred, we are walking around in a state of spiritual death. In fact in the same verse, it says that, "the grasshopper drags himself along." What a view of a person with no desire! *Just dragging himself along, just existing*! But with desire he becomes like Paul in Philippians 3:14 where he is "reaching toward his goal!" Our goal and our desire are to go deeper and further into this anointing!!!

CHAPTER 10

BEYOND ALL THAT I CAN ASK OR THINK

GOD CAN DO ANYTHING IF HE CAN GET US TO AGREE

This immense statement actually comes from the verse that follows the promise of fullness in Ephesians 3:20 KJV. "Now unto him that is able to do exceeding abundantly above all that we can ask or think, according to the power that worketh in us." It shows how God works!

What is God saying? He can do anything if He can get us into agreement. So how does He get us there? He touches us with vision! Vision is actually part of the language of the Holy Spirit. In Joel 2:28, when the promise of the outpouring of the Spirit is given, we are promised that there would be dreams and visions to both young and old. On the day of Pentecost, Peter actually quotes this whole passage in Acts 2:16-21. He was letting us know that God prophesied it and now had outpoured it. This meant that the time of the dreams and visions had come into fulfillment in this great outpouring!

TURNED INTO VISIONARIES

The Holy Spirit, as part of His ministry in us, causes us to become visionaries. In Proverbs 29:18, we are told that where there is no vision there is no direction, no purpose and basic nakedness. Why? Because vision is the driving force of our life! A young man or woman with no vision will not apply themselves to study. They will wander aimlessly. A Christian with no vision will be purposeless, but when touched by the Spirit, vision and dreams will be stirred. Paul speaks of this in Philippians 3:12-14. "But I press on to take hold of that for which Christ Jesus took hold of me. Brothers I do not consider myself to have taken hold of it. But one thing I do: Forgetting what is behind and straining to what is ahead, I press on toward the goal to win the prize for which God has called me heavenward in Christ Jesus," (NIV 1984 version). He makes it clear that the driving force in his life is the vision that had possessed his life. In fact, in chapter 3:12, he uses the same Greek word Katalambanō. We used this in our previous chapter to speak of taking hold of or grasping, but this time it took hold of him so that he, in turn, would take hold of it! This is key to what the Lord wants to do, which is get His vision in us so that we desire to possess it for ourselves.

ASKING BECOMES A KEY

Now we step into the second part of this great verse. Not only do we think or envision but we ASK! We now press in like Paul and begin to agree with the Lord's promptings. We start to ask for what we feel, see and know that we are supposed to possess. Paul's example is clear. In Genesis 32:24-29, Jacob gives us

41

the same example of pressing in until he's possessed. One thing was a promise while another thing was a possession. In fact, in verse 26 his asking moved into a demand. "I will not let you go unless." Oh, how I love it! We must want it so much that the word no doesn't mean no. It means ask again and again and again. In 2 Kings 2:9, Elijah asked Elisha what he wanted. We have got to want and really want it in order to reach in for all that is ours. Read the whole passage. Not only did he want it, but he was prepared to go the extra mile to get it. Now that is wanting! That is asking and demanding!

He is able to do more than vision or asking according to our promise. He is able to do according to His power within us. The river is waiting to explode in us and on us, my friends!

CHAPTER 11

THE MINISTRY OF THE HOLY SPIRIT

If ever a chapter in the Bible stirred anyone, then this is the chapter that stirs me. It is the chapter in which the ministry of the Spirit is explained, which is 2 Corinthians 3. What a revelation of all that the Spirit does and how He ministers. Then the crown of all crowns wants to share His ministry with us! It is the part of His ministry linked to this book that I want to share.

MANIFESTED GLORY

The Holy Spirit's ministry is one of manifested glory! In fact, so great is this glory that Paul speaks of it this way in 2 Corinthians 3:8-10. "Will not the ministry of the Spirit be even more glorious? If the ministry that brought condemnation was glorious, how much more glorious is the ministry that brings righteousness! For what was glorious has no glory now in comparison with the surpassing glory."

Now that is glory indeed! When you are thinking that the comparison is that of the glory of God that touched Mount Sinai in Exodus 19, that also made Moses' face shine with glory in Exodus 34:29. What a glory! But this ministry far surpasses that. The Holy Spirit is none other than the revealer of the glory of God! Not just in a general sense, but we find in this great chapter that He wants to reveal it to us! 2 Corinthians 3:18 ESV shares this great truth. "And we all, with unveiled face, beholding the glory of the Lord." What is this great verse saying? It is saying that the Holy Spirit takes the veil of non-understanding off us and reveals the glory of the Lord to us. This verse gets even more shocking! "Are being transformed into the same image from one degree of glory to another."

TRANSFORMED FROM GLORY TO GLORY

So the Holy Spirit reveals to us God's glory one step at a time so that as we see it, we are transformed by it and then walk into what is revealed. In fact, one version says that not only do we see it and gain it, but we also reflect it. Now listen to the promise from the, "And we all." And what? "We all." (See 2 Cor. 3:18) That means that this ministry is for all and to all. The Holy Spirit wants to lead us all into the fullness of God's glory. That's His mission, ministry and purpose to us and through us. In 2 Corinthians 4:1, Paul then explains that he personally, has had this ministry of the Spirit to him and through him. "Therefore, seeing we have this ministry, as we have received mercy."

TREASURE IN EARTHEN VESSELS

Notice he uses the word we. It's not just for him, but it is for us. Another translation actually says, "Since through God's mercy we have this ministry." This means all that receive God's mercy can also be participants in this great ministry! That, my friends, means us. Later, in the same chapter in verse 7, Paul tells us that, "We carry this treasure in earthen vessels." The manifestation of the revealed glory of God carried around in these weak vessels. Wow, it has always been the purpose of the Lord to reveal Christ in us and through us!

THE JOURNEY OF HIS MINISTRY IN US

The ministry of the Spirit started when He, like a lion of Judah, hounded us to gain us. Then when born again, He placed Himself, the Spirit of Christ, in us (Rom. 8:9). This was the beginning of the good work of fullness that is found in Philippians 1:6. "He that began the good work in you, will carry it to completion, until the day of Christ Jesus," (NIV 1984 version).

CHAPTER 12

HOW GOD USES PEOPLE TO SPUR US ON

When Paul makes the statement to the Romans that he would come in the full measure of Christ in Roman 15:29, it probably did several things to them. Firstly, it created an expectancy. Wow! Perhaps God will meet me or touch me when Paul comes. Secondly, when they saw it in manifestation, they would be stirred to want it in their lives. Ephesians 4:13 tells us that the ministry of the "Doma" gifts of God would lead us to fullness or full measure.

THE STORY OF MY LIFE

This has been the story of my life since being born again. Watching my first pastor and his anointing stirred me to want more. Then reading of Smith Wigglesworth and other greats in the faith did the same. Kathryn Kuhlman's books stirred me beyond measure. When Benny Hinn came into England the first time, the affect was so powerful on me and stirred a cry to want to know the Holy Spirit in the same way. Out of all the stirrings, which are so many, perhaps the greatest was when I met a man while on vacation in Europe. The anointing and the measure of his walk in God was staggering! I remember the impact to this day when a cry came out of my spirit, "I must have it! I must have it!" No, the cry wasn't generated by him but by the Holy Spirit Himself as He used another's anointing to release a longing so deep in me. I actually had to run away from the group of people I was with to cry out to the Lord in longing and almost anguish.

THE ANOINTING INCREASES

With so many of these experiences I have walked, there are definite times that I encountered an exponential increase of the measure of the anointing. I remember being in a hotel in a small town in Texas when someone gave me a tape of a testimony of a known gift ministry. Once again, the cry came. I met the Lord that day after hours of prayer and what an increase of the measure of the anointing. It poured out wherever I went. Several years later, I again felt a cry within my heart to encounter the Lord afresh. While praying for such an experience, I read a book by Bill Johnson about his encounter. It thrust me deeper into my quest and the results were life changing to not only myself, but anybody that I ministered to after this period. These encounters can come in person, by testimony, in a book, by listening to a recording or when hands are laid upon you. There is no doubt that God uses these anointed ones to take you to greater measures.

NO MISTAKES IN GOD

I believe intensely that the Lord, who sets out the map of our life, and the Spirit, who guides our steps, can cause us to run into the anointed person who is our *crossroads*. This experience can take us to the next phase or level of our life. This can come as a one off encounter or a season of walking together. We need to ask the Lord in prayer constantly that we run into the people of destiny that will help us move further up the river of God.

FATHERING

As we study Galatians 4 and so many other places in the scripture, the Lord speaks of bringing us to maturity by others that have walked before us. This is called, *fathering,* a God ordained method of growth and discipleship. Look at Joshua, Elisha and Timothy for examples. These spiritual fathers, and of course mothers, teach us and help raise us up in Christ, but with the ultimate aim of impartation from their walk with God into ours. No one can read about the anointing coming to Elisha without seeing this most incredible provision of the Lord. The desire was created by the Lord, but he came through the walk with his spiritual father. I always look for those who walk in arenas I haven't to learn and gain from them. It has been my experience to find so many in my life. What a provision from the Lord! What a place to grow and receive impartation! It is irreplaceable in our journey into more.

My prayer for myself even now, is that the Lord will draw me to those He wants me to gain from in whatever form He deems necessary. It actually excites me to see who is next.

He won't stop until he fulfills the purpose of God! We must open ourselves to His ministry, both to us, in us and then through us! Truly, let's cry for the unveiled face promised in 2 Corinthians 3:18 and be moved from glory to glory.

CHAPTER 13

DEALING WITH STAGNANCY

One of the greatest hindrances to growth in measure is dealing with stagnancy. Ezekiel 47 mentions quite clearly that while following the growth of the river of God, there is a troubled area alongside the river. In the NIV version, it speaks three different times of the freshness caused by the river, but suddenly an unfresh dead area is spoken of (see Eze. 47:8-11). The area occupied by the marshes in verse 11. There is no freshness found there, just stagnancy and staleness! There is no fresh water, flow or life pouring through. Here there is no fruit tree, just that stench of stagnant water. We might get a few frogs but certainly no freshwater fish. What causes these marsh places when the river is easy to access?

1. Having a disconnect with the life of the river. The best it can do is wait for an overflow. It either didn't follow the flow or disconnected itself along the way. This can come from religion rather than life, but also neglect or laziness in the Christian walk. Perhaps it comes from the undealt with areas of the heart as warned in Proverbs 4:23.
2. An unrepentant heart will also cut off the flow of the life of God. Ephesians 4:18 speaks of this saying, "the hardening of the heart, can cut off the life of God."
3. Another is futile thinking, which we find in verse 17 of the same chapter. This can be translated as

50

4. pointless and senseless. This is worldly, carnal and self-centered thinking that has not allowed itself to be transformed according to Romans 12:2. We fight a spirit of narcissism today in our society and it wars against the church walking into its destiny. Is your thinking causing stagnancy instead of life?

5. A loss of thirst is another reason that the church can become stagnant. David, who clearly was a man of the Spirit, continually pens his longing and thirst. Psalms 63 is an awesome depiction of this. The longing and thirst overflows into active pursuance. "My soul follows hard after you," (See Ps. 63:8 KJV). Time doesn't allow us to speak of all David's touches, anointing and revelations. He wanted everything and surely walked in it. Do we thirst for God's fullness, or have we become stagnant?

6. Complacency is another reason for stagnancy. In Song of Solomon 3:1 this is clearly shown. "All night long on my bed I looked for the one my heart loves; I looked for him but did not find him." She expected him to come to where she was but refused to follow him to where he wanted her to be! His answer was to pull away and draw her into a new place. Complacency causes marshland Christianity.

7. Another reason is having no revelation of either the purpose or provision of God. I remember going to church from the time I was a baby until I hit about 16. I caught religion and a knowing that God existed but never a thought that I could be filled with the Spirit to overflowing. Then I got born again in a good old fashioned Pentecostal church

that was led by a man of the Spirit. He once told me, "I was born in the fire so I would never want anything but the fire." *He was right!* Why? Because a revelation for purpose and inheritance was released to me. Paul speaks of this in Ephesians 1:17-19. This is a summary of what he said. You need revelation of who God is, revelation of what is available and revelation of the power of God toward you. Why was he telling them? Because they needed to get out of the marshes. They needed to get into the river in its fullness, but without the revelation of it they never would. We were called to be filled to fullness Christians, not stagnant lifeless ones. "Lead me further up the river," we cry once again.

CONCLUSION

Cleary following Paul the writer of much of the New Testament, he shows a quest to know God more and possess more of God. His famous passage in Philippians 3 Verses 8-15, is clearly a huge encouragement to want more and desire more and follow after more. It starts with being met by Christ to wanting more of Christ to chasing and pressing in to have more of Christ. Surely if Paul wanted more and gained more, shouldn't we? But it is not just limited to Paul, there is Peter and John and David of the Old Testament, the number is limitless. We were saved to have all that God has for us and to walk in his fullness. As one great preacher said,' Further up the river and the river further up me!'

There is more and we should want more and chase more. Hence the reason for this book.

TESTIMONIES

"My friend Dennis Goldsworthy-Davis is known for being hard-hitting, straight-shooting and uncompromising in his preaching, teaching and prophetic ministry. You will find his writing to be the same! I love how he creatively challenges us to break free from old religious mindsets to embrace God's increased measures of the anointing in our lives! In his new book: There Must Be More - Pursuing the Ever Increasing Anointing, Dennis gives us a clear vision of a restored lifestyle walking in the anointing. He gives us rich insights surrounding our personal and corporate walk with God. Dennis takes us on a journey toward restoring a New Testament manifestation of the anointing. You will be challenged and inspired!"

Dr. Greg Hood, Th.D.
Author of: The Gospel of the Kingdom; Rebuilding the Broken Altar; Sonship According to the Kingdom; and Citizenship According to the Kingdom
Apostolic Overseer - The Network of Five-Fold Ministers and Churches Founder and President of Kingdom University and Greg Hood Ministries
www.GregHood.org www.KingdomU.org

"My friend Dennis Goldsworthy Davis has penned what we have all known [but were hesitant to admit] There Has To Be More! The "More" that Dennis outlines is not how to get more money, recognition, or promotion – but how to walk

in the very thing that fulfills John 3:30, "He must increase, but I must decrease." If we're honest, most of us [who minister the Word] know what it is like to attempt to minister the Power of the Holy Spirit from an empty vessel. There is nothing lonelier than trying to minister the Word of God without the anointing, and nothing more exciting than allowing God to work through those who have yielded to His ever-increasing anointing. There is one statement in particular that Dennis made that captured my attention straight way and drove me into a deeper desire for more was - The desire for all that God has for us must become such a longing that it will drive us into action—the action that will stop at nothing to be fulfilled and until we become filled to overflowing.

Other books have been written about the anointing, but what's different about There Has To Be More is that it comes from a man who knows from whence he speaks! This is not another book on "Ten Easy Steps to the Anointing," but it comes from deep within a heart that says, "I want more, and I am going to have more because that is my inheritance too."

My sincere desire for all who read this book is when you finish reading, stop, and cry out to God and declare, "There Has To Be More," I will not stop until I have it!"

Dr. J. Tod Zeiger
President, Tod Zeiger Ministries
Friendsville, Tennessee 37737

BIOGRAPHY

Dennis Paul Goldsworthy-Davis has been blessed to travel extensively throughout the world ministering both apostolically and prophetically to the body of Christ. He operates within a strong governmental prophetic office and frequently sees the Presence of God and the Spirit of Revival break out upon the lives of people. Dennis has equally been graced to relate to many spiritual sons throughout the earth, bringing wisdom, guidance and encouragement.

Printed in Great Britain
by Amazon

27125270R00036